What A Blind Dog Sees

J. Bradfield McConnell

Outskirts Press, Inc.
http://www.outskirtspress.com

ISBN: 978-1-4327-9797-3

Outskirts Press and the "OP" logo are trademarks belonging to Outskirts Press, Inc.

PRINTED IN THE UNITED STATES OF AMERICA

To Jackson for being such a great and inspiring dog.
To Collie Rescue of the Carolinas for taking good care of Jackson
until we could adopt him.
In loving memory of her dog Clyde,
many thanks to Rita J. Simmons for her wonderful illustrations.
And to my wife, Gloria for all of her help and encouragement.
—J. Bradfield McConnell

This Book Belongs to:

To Katy & Sarah,
Best Wishes,
J.B. Mofuell

This is Jackson and he was born blind,
But he's not worried. He doesn't even mind.

He does what dogs do, but it's fair to say
Like all blind dogs, Jackson has his own way.

If you saw him at home I doubt you would know.
When he's chasing his brothers you should see him go!

If you watch Jackson closely it soon becomes plain—
He kicks his paws forward like he's using a cane.

He uses his whiskers, his fur, and his ears
To form a mental picture of what he feels and hears.

When Jackson was young he chewed up my socks,
But his favorite game was killing a box!

Jackson loves brushing, playtime, and treats,
And he burps quite loudly right after he eats.

And would you believe it? He loves to eat ice!
It helps keep his teeth very shiny and nice.

He romps with two Huskies who play very rough,
But run away quickly when Jackson's had enough.

He groans and snores when he is asleep.
Like seeing Collies he even herds sheep!

Yet most of his herding, at least so far,
Is herding his people toward the treat jar.

Jackson helps people when they're in need.
He listens to kids who are learning to read.

He goes to a rest home where old people stay.
He stops there to greet them and brighten their day!

With three doggie brothers, his Mom and his Dad,
Jackson has the best life a dog ever had.

And when I'm with Jackson, down on my knees
With my arms around him and I give him a squeeze—
Well, that's when I know what a blind dog sees.

❧ The End ❧

CPSIA information can be obtained
at www.ICGtesting.com
Printed in the USA
LVIW012223051112

306015LV00002B